The Maple Crew

A Memoir

The Maple Crew

A Memoir

By

Jessie Maple

With E. Danielle Butler

Copyright © 2019 by Jessie Maple

All rights reserved. This book or any portion thereof may not be reproduced or used in any manner whatsoever without the express written permission of the publisher except for the use of brief quotations in a book review.

Jessie Maple jessiemaplebooks@aol.com

EvyDani Books, LLC hello@evydanibooks.com

Cover Photos: Leroy Patton
Photos courtesy of Leroy Patton and pulled from Jessie Maple's private collection.
Cover Design: Latonia Burgess, LKB Designs & Photography
Editing: Windy Goodloe, Nzadi Amistad Editing & Writing Services
Interior: Tara Culton, OnTime Tasks

Library of Congress Cataloging Information Available
ISBN: 978-0-5785-0202-1

Printed in the United States of America

Disclaimer

This work depicts actual events in the life of the author as truthfully as recollection permits and/or can be verified by research. Occasionally, dialogue consistent with the character or nature of the person speaking has been supplemented. All persons within are actual individuals; there are no composite characters. The names of some individuals have been changed to respect their privacy.

Table of Contents

Disclaimer iv

Introduction .... - 1 -

PART 1: GETTING STARTED

Kinship .... - 6 -

Bacteriology and the Lab .... - 13 -

Unsatisfied .... - 17 -

City Living and Sacrifice .... - 19 -

A Love Story .... - 22 -

Secretly Married and Repercussions .... - 27 -

Choosing Journalism .... - 29 -

Broadcast Journalism .... - 32 -

The Apprentice .... - 35 -

Choosing the Union .... - 38 -

The Trial Period .... - 40 -

Queasy Helicopters and Other Secrets .... - 41 -

Cat Nibbles and Comb-Overs .... - 44 -

Big Stories .... - 47 -

In All the Frames .... - 51 -

Carry the Heavy Load .... - 52 -

Fun in the Spotlight .... - 55 -

From News to Film .... - 57 -

Good Music and Private Parties .... - 59 -

PART 2: GAINING MY INDEPENDENCE

Feature Films and Documentaries .... - 62 -

20 West .... - 69 -

More Than Movies .... - 74 -

On Friendship .... - 76 -

On Fantasies and Good Times .... - 83 -

PART 3: LESSONS AND HIGHLIGHTS

Maple Crew Values .... - 86 -

Cookies and Other Money Makers .... - 94 -

Firsts .... - 97 -

Archives and Honors .... - 99 -

New Generation Daughters and Sons .... - 106 -

With All Due Respect .... - 108 -

Next Scenes and Rolling Credits .... - 110 -

PART 4: MY PHOTO MEMORIES 120

Acknowledgements – Jessie Maple .... - 120 -

Acknowledgements – E. Danielle Butler .... - 121 -

Works of Jessie Maple .... - 123 -

Image Index .... - 125 -

About the Author .... - 128 -

About the Co-Author .... - 129 -

INTRODUCTION

I released my first book, *How to Become a Union Camerawoman – Film, Video Tape,* in 1977, with no intention of being an author. However, I'd accomplished something and thought it worth documenting for others. I shared my journey about becoming the first black woman accepted into the unionized film industry in 1974. The book was written to be a guide for the young black and other minority women that were reaching out to me for advice. If I hadn't written the book, I'd have had a stack of unanswered mail from women who looked like me and, in some cases, wanted to be like me. It seemed necessary to share my experience with those that would ultimately walk the path I'd laid.

In the book, I candidly shared the challenges that I had faced in my own career which ultimately led to me being accepted in the union. I wasn't trying to be the first; I was simply trying to get what was fair for me – an opportunity. Abusive and discriminatory practices were a part of my experience, and I did not believe it was necessary for other women to have to endure those same challenges. In the book, I shared details on becoming a camerawoman, joining a union, and highlighted other jobs within the film industry. I even provided resources for finding work and contact information for local film unions. The book was quite technical in nature and offered an educational, albeit historical, account of the film and emerging video industry at the time.

While I would like to think that the intention and guidance with which I wrote the book were the primary draw, that was not the case. In *How to Become a Union Camerawoman*, I shared my courageous (termed crazy by others) choice to file a complaint against three television networks, but I pursued the case against the local WCBS network for racial and sexual discrimination. My initial claim was rejected on the grounds of no probable cause by the City of New York Commission on Human Rights. I filed an appeal, shared documents from the pending case, and described the discriminatory practices in the book itself. At the time, the traditional publishing houses were not looking for books like mine. I also didn't want to wait on their approval or changes either. Instead, I hired an editor and published the book myself. My husband, Leroy, and I commissioned an ambitious print run of five thousand copies of the work. (The book is out of print now, though I toy with the idea of rereleasing it sometime in the near future.) Just before the self-published book went to press, I received news that my WCBS appeal had been approved. Eleanor Holmes Norton ordered my case reopened for further investigation. Ms. Norton is now a US congresswoman. I say a little prayer each time I see her name or face.

As the commission reviewed my case for the second time, my stakes were even higher. Aside from having money on the line, my reputation and dream of becoming a camerawoman were at stake. I'd parted ways with my first husband and, no doubt, had shaken my daughter's life up from what she'd known up until that point. Needless to say, my stress level was high as I anxiously awaited their decision. My attorney advised me to take a vacation, as there wasn't much that either of us could do while the commission deliberated.

The Maple Crew

This book, *The Maple Crew,* picks up at that time and sheds light on my life as it unfolded. While there are many things that played out in the public eye, there were several other angles unfolding behind the lens. I also share more about my upbringing and personal life, so you can see how it all came together.

The list of my work includes feature films, short films, documentaries, commercials, and music videos. I have completed many documentaries in my time, but I am a storyteller at heart. You will find that the action captured here aligns more with the latter in many ways.

I Believe.

Jessie Maple, 2019

Jessie Maple

PART 1:
GETTING STARTED

The Maple Crew

Figure 1 My birth and childhood home

9/21/2019
To Mike + Shelbey
I believe
Jessie Maple

KINSHIP

My roots are in Mississippi, but most people associate me with my life in New York. I was born into a large family with seven brothers and four sisters. My mother had two sets of children, and I was the second oldest of the first six.

Lost Father and Brother

My daddy is my favorite man, though I only knew him for less than fourteen years. Daddy was a good man. He didn't gamble or drink alcohol. He worked hard and provided for his family. When I met a man, I had someone to compare them with.

My father and his brothers, along with cousins and other men in the family, were farmers and long-distance truck drivers. They picked cotton, raised crops, and maintained livestock. I remember them closing out the crops at the end of each season. After picking the cotton, they'd take it to the town to sell. Looking back, when my parents went to town, it was only to buy shoes, flour, cornmeal, molasses, and sugar. Everything else we needed, we produced on our own. It seems that independence and sustainability run in my blood.

The death of my father was the hardest thing that I ever had to go

Figure 2 Me and my 'simmon tree

through. I was a daddy's girl. It took me a long time to get over it; but, getting past losing him helped me get through a lot of trials and tribulations later in life. I had to stay focused. Even though I had a lot of uncles and other family, no one could take my daddy's place. I had to get through that experience.

Daddy said something to me once when he was dragging me on his cotton sack that has stuck with me my entire life. He said, "If I have anything when I leave this world, I will leave it to Jessie because she will know what to do with it." He saw that in me early on, so I wasn't trying to prove that to him as I went through life. I just wanted to do good for myself.

When Daddy was alive, he gave me a persimmon tree. Persimmons were a big thing in the area where we were raised; I was happy to have something to call my own. My siblings weren't allowed to take the fruit unless they had permission from me. Although I didn't know anything about what meditation was at the time, the 'simmon tree became my meditation place. I would sit under the tree and think with no one bothering me. With my imagination running free, I'd play in the dirt and contemplate whatever images where appearing in my mind's eye. I was meditating and planning before understanding the power of either. After Daddy's passing, I'd sit under the tree to feel a sense of connection to him.

Daddy's family didn't take any responsibility to help my mother or to help us after he died. My siblings and I were not seen as most likely to succeed. At that time, in my community, the boys only went to school up to the eighth grade, and then they'd go out to work with their fathers. That happened to my older brother, and then my father died. When my father died, I think it was like my oldest brother died, too, even though he lived a long time after that.

Mother's Manners

When people ask where I got my manners, I quickly tell them that I learned from my parents, particularly my mother. My mother had a way about herself, and I was able to pick up many things. She came from an educated family. In her generation, and those before her, if you made it to the eighth grade, you were considered skilled enough to hold certain jobs. My mother made it through the eighth grade and became a teacher. There was no Board of Education with rules and regulations. They used the knowledge that the people in the community had. I continue to use the same premise in my work today. Now, I say, "Invest in your community."

My mother married young, at age sixteen, and became a housewife. She didn't know anything about fieldwork, picking cotton, or other kinds of physical labor. Her job was to take care of the kids. She'd cook, wash, make dresses for the girls, and keep the house clean.

When my father died, my mother had never had an independent life.

Figure 3 Me in one of Mommy's suits

She went searching, I suppose, for that. She discovered a whole new life and went for it. I was thirteen and my oldest brother was sixteen when my mother gathered us together and asked us what we wanted her to do with the land that my father had left us. She didn't know what to do with it, and neither did we. We were so sad, and we just wanted our mother to do what she thought was best. We told her, "Do what makes you happy." And, boy, did she do it! She sold the property and bought a fabulous house on Summit Street in McComb, Mississippi. It was just down from the town hall, where all the affluent Blacks used to gather for good times. It was the only hall in McComb where Blacks could dress in their party clothes and enjoy blues concerts with the likes of B.B. King and Etta James.

I learned how to dress from my mother. After she left the country, she dressed fabulously! She'd wear those man-tailored suits, which were popular back then. A white one and a beige one were the ones that I vividly remember. The jackets came down below her waistline, and the skirts were straight. I said, "Mommy, save me those suits!" And she saved them for me to wear when I got older. Whatever she had, it was the best, her clothing and everything else.

My parents taught me how to make a living. I can say now that I got my upbringing from my mother and my father. I'm independent and work for myself because that's what I saw. You have to work for yourself, make your own decisions, and not make anyone else responsible for your success or shortcomings. I also learned to enjoy the good things that life had to offer from my mother.

Later, when I experienced struggles, my mother was right there with me. She understood that what I was doing was important. As my career flourished, I would take her to some of the functions I was a part of. She came with me to celebrate the last award I received from the New York Foundation for the Arts. While we were at the ceremony, she said, "One half of the world don't know what the other half is doing," because she hadn't been to anything like that before. I just let her enjoy herself.

Figure 4 Mommy and me

Sweet Sisterhood

I have one sister, Peggy, that I am very close to. In fact, she's more than a sister; she's a great friend. I've shared practically everything with her, good, bad, ugly, and indifferent. We've been through so much together that I could share many stories. However, there is one that I think sums up the depth and breadth of our relationship quite well.

Figure 5 My sister Peggy

One year, my husband, Leroy, and I found ourselves alone in New York for the Thanksgiving holiday. We did not have much money at the time, so the outlook was pretty bleak for celebrating at all. When I spoke with my sister in advance of that Thursday, I knew she could hear the disappointment in my voice. She was in South Carolina, and I was in New York, so there really was nothing that could be done, or so I thought. On Thanksgiving Day, just as Leroy and I were preparing to have our sad meal, Peggy called me and instructed, "Meet the four pm train at Penn Station." Imagine my surprise to find that my sister had neatly packed an entire Thanksgiving dinner and shipped it to us! Everything was there — corn bread, pies, beans, greens and all the other trimmings. Her husband, Fred, exclaimed, "I've never seen anybody ship corn bread to New York on a train!" I have no idea how that food stayed so neat after traveling that distance. Leroy and I had a perfect Thanksgiving thanks to her love and ingenuity. I have so many more stories like that, about how Peggy has been with me over the years. But I think this one makes me smile the biggest when I think about it.

Figure 6 Peggy & Fred

BACTERIOLOGY AND THE LAB

After high school, I wanted to be a doctor, but I realized that I wasn't prepared for what it would take to get there. However, after some research, I discovered the medical technology field. I could wear the white lab coat and help other people. Once I completed my education in medical technology, I started my professional career as a lab technician in bacteriology.

When I began, there weren't that many Blacks in the field. And the ones that were there were employed in the hematology lab. They saved the bacteriology lab for flunked-out doctors. It was a privileged lab, and that was where I wanted to work. Plus, I was good at bacteriology and didn't like hematology enough to want to pursue it as a career.

I make a comparison between Blacks and hematology and the privilege of bacteriology for whites when I talk about entering the film industry. They, often, tried to steer women into editing. They figured we couldn't do the other jobs. After I got my training, I realized, Oh, this is one of those things they have special for women. Women go into editing. I compare them because of how there were specific areas designated for minorities, of color and gender. I did not want to be confined to those spaces, especially since I was capable of performing the duties. In both cases, I made my way to take up the space I deserved.

Lunchtime Work

I prayed for a job where I'd be in a supervisory role, so I could be good to my people. I was given that job in the bacteriology lab. I helped get the last hospital that I worked for unionized before I really knew what a union was. On my lunch hour, I would go out and picket with what they called "the little people." The other big-shot technicians and doctors would ask, "Can she do that?" And then someone would say, "She does what she wants to do. She's on her lunch hour!" I took full advantage of the freedom.

Leading the Lab

I was the head of the lab for about three years while they were searching for a doctor. You're supposed to have a PhD in order to hold the lead role, but I was so good that they just took their time filling the position.

Figure 7 Me with my coworkers at the lab

Some workers spent their time complaining in the bathroom about how they were being treated or what they weren't getting. It didn't make sense to me, for someone to spend their time complaining, instead of going to ask for things directly. When I thought I should get a raise, I went straight to Dr. Dolphin, the head doctor over the hospital, and said, "I want a raise." His response was, "Well, you've got a title. You're the head of the lab." I told him, "Yeah, but I can't go around the corner and buy a loaf of bread with a title." He gave me my raise, but he told me not to tell anyone else. I came out talking loud and said, "I got my raise. You better go get yours." They thought I'd lost my mind! There was one woman on the team that I wanted to get her a raise also, but I knew that she wasn't bold enough to ask for it directly. She'd just continue to talk about her dissatisfaction in the bathroom. Part of the reason for my talking loud was to help and to encourage her, too. I was good to all my people. In fact, I focused a lot of energy on making sure that people were treated fairly and received the same consideration for their work ability.

Due Credit

During my tenure supervising the lab, I was given credit for the discovery of an unidentified microorganism. I was responsible for doing the research once we determined that the bacteria we'd found hadn't been listed in any medical journals. The strains were related to *Achromobacter* and *Moraxella*. This acknowledgement for the Hospital for Joint Diseases and Medical Center Bacteriology Lab under my direction was cited in the *American Society for Microbiology* journal.

Figure 8 lab journal recognition

When I decided to leave the lab after nearly six years, I'd left an indelible mark. It was likely that I could have continued that path if I desired. However, I wasn't sure what was next. I just knew that it was time to go.

UNSATISFIED

I was married with a beautiful baby girl and a great job as a bacteriologist with supervisory responsibilities. We had a nice apartment. I had my own car and took care of home life.

My first husband couldn't understand what more I could want. Yet there I was, wanting more. I'd already done the seemingly impossible in my medical career and was ready for a new endeavor. I had it good, but I knew there was better. While my ex-husband was comfortable, I grew increasingly uncomfortable. Finally, I made the difficult decision to seek my own satisfaction.

For a long time, I wanted to change my profession, but because I had to work and help support my family, I was not able to stop working until later. After being in the medical field for six years, I was not satisfied with what I was doing, looking at those little bacteria every day. Yes, it was a secure profession, but my time was up. My boss even asked me to stay on another six months. They finally found a PhD to head the lab after I had filled the position for more than two years. I was required to tell the staff that I wasn't in charge anymore because they, initially, didn't believe the news about the change.

I had saved enough money for my daughter, Audrey, and me to make it on our own for three months. I had an agent contact at the time that could help me go back to work if I needed to. With that three months' worth of savings, I was well protected and had time to look around and decide what I wanted to do.

CITY LIVING AND SACRIFICE

Since I lived right in the city, in Manhattan, I didn't want my daughter Audrey to go to public school. I'd experienced the public schools in the north with my brothers and sisters. Being from the south, our first teachers were cousins and other family members. There was a level of love and attention that accompanied the discipline. We knew they cared about us. However, after transferring to school in the north, it felt as though we just became a number. I had been sheltered for a good portion of my upbringing, so much so, that I was scared to even use the bathroom in Philadelphia. I'd literally get off the bus and run home. The other girls that were my age were smoking and cursing; I had to pass by them, afraid. In my mind, that was grown-up behavior. After completing my last year of high school in the north, I knew what the exposure was like, and I didn't want that for Audrey. My desire for her to go to private school caused a little conflict between her father and me. We disagreed, so if I wanted her to go to private school, I was going to have to pay for it. I had to take responsibility for my daughter. I was working two jobs, so being a part of the PTA wasn't an option. It was up to me to find a school that was compatible for me and Audrey.

Figure 9 Audrey's senior yearbook page

I wanted more for Audrey. Her schooling and her needing more was one of the whys behind my quest for success. I needed to provide better for her. I needed to provide safety for her. I needed to provide options for her. I made the decision to enroll Audrey in private school. I was blessed enough through much work and many sacrifices that she was able to attend private school from three years old through high school graduation. Of course, there were some days when I wasn't sure where the money was going to come from, but I always believed that it would come – and it did. The sacrifice paid off when she earned entry into Syracuse University and obtained a dual degree in accounting and speech communication.

Figure 10 Audrey & me

Observant Onlooker

A lot was happening in our world. I did not know that Audrey had noticed everything that was going on. She knew that it was not easy for me. When I took the union test for the first time and didn't pass, I cried and cried. I called my sister Peggy, and she came and cried with me. Audrey saw all those moments, but she didn't act like it. I found out just how much Audrey had observed when it was time for her to go to college. In one of her entrance essays, she wrote about the things she had seen me endure.

Figure 11 Me, Audrey, Peggy, & Mommy

A Love Story

If my current husband, Leroy Patton, were writing this, the entire book would be a love story. You've probably noticed by now that I'm quite independent. One of the great things about our marriage is that he lets me be independent. So, I'll tell the story of our marriage my way for now.

I certainly wasn't looking for anyone when he came into my life. And someone in the industry was absolutely out of the question. I was on a quest to develop my second career.

There was a five-year stretch between my first and second marriage. I had a daughter. I didn't date and entertain men in front of her. I didn't believe in living with men. Leroy had his own apartment, and I had mine. When I first met him, he was a big-time still photographer with *Jet* and *Ebony* living in Los Angeles. *Jet* and *Ebony* were divisions of the Black media conglomerate, Johnson Publications, a prominent news and entertainment outlet. He wanted me to move out west, but I said, "No. I'm staying in New York."

Well, that's it! That's our love story, my version of it anyway. I'm sure that, because I am a filmmaker, you were expecting a few more details from me. Let me share the made-for-the-movies version of our relationship.

The Maple Crew

I was freelancing for a New York magazine when I met Leroy. The bosses at the magazine had sent me to California with all the digs – hotel, chauffer, great food, whatever I needed, so I could focus on my work. This particular assignment also carried me to Texas to cover a movie. A dear friend of mine, who was also serving as a guide, was unable to accompany me at the time, so he reached out to Leroy and asked him to meet me. My friend knew that I wouldn't leave the hotel and do any exploring.

When Leroy arrived at my hotel room and saw me, he was taken with me. He said I was "Vaseline clean" because I didn't wear make-up. Leroy took pictures of me immediately. With high hopes, he let me know that we'd meet up the next day.

Figure 12 Leroy Patton's first photograph of me

Leroy gave me his number in hopes that I would call. In his mind, he believed, if I called, that would mean I was interested. He called me. We began to visit back-and-forth to New York, where I lived, and California where he was planted. Somehow or another, a bi-coastal relationship developed. Although we'd evolved, I think the deal was officially sealed when I made an overnight visit to Las Vegas to surprise him for his birthday.

Met with Resistance

I know that our whirlwind love story sounds like something out of a movie. After all, we were both beginning our film careers. But don't think that our love wasn't met with challenges. It was … how do the kids say it today? Complicated. Yeah, it was complicated. My focus was on my career, but I didn't mention that I was also separated from my first husband. That wasn't the most dramatic part though. Imagine my surprise when my girlfriend Carol called me to tell me that my new beau was married! She'd found out through a *Jet* magazine interview he'd done. In the article, Leroy had mentioned being in bed with his wife when an earthquake hit.

I'd fallen for him already. By the time his interview was released, it was too late for my heart. Things were tough. I was accused of breaking up a home and a family. There were phone calls. His wife called me. Her girlfriends called me. Thankfully, the times of social media and gossip segments hadn't arrived yet. There was nowhere else for it to go except for the telephone. Our complicated situation would have been a hot headliner in the entertainment section. Fortunately, we made it through without too much embarrassment for ourselves or our families.

Figure 13 Leroy & me

Broken Hearts

My family didn't know about me and Leroy until I divorced and got married. Then, I told them because I was "Sweet Jessie," and I wasn't sure what their reaction would be. And I was still Sweet Jessie. Things just happened. It was an upsetting time for me because I couldn't tell them. I cried for a couple of months because my first husband was an only child, and I was like his mother's daughter. The loss of my relationship with his mother was very hurtful to me. I couldn't be friends with her and continue to act like her daughter because it wasn't fair, so I just broke off the whole thing. I don't regret it. My daughter might still be mad, but I don't regret it. I needed that time.

Leroy and I both were divorced at eleven in the morning and married at three in the afternoon in a small church in the Dominican Republic. We thought we could have a honeymoon (I guess you could call it that), but we had only booked to stay there two nights. We got married, and when our two nights were up, they put us out immediately because they were having a fiesta.

What I've Learned About Marriage

It's been decades since Leroy and I wed. We've seen our share of things both within relationship to ourselves, each other, and in relation to the outside world. I don't want everybody to think that being married is all candy. There's some bitter chocolate that goes with it. I've worked faithfully to keep my second marriage together. I don't want to experience the kind of hurt that I did before, for myself or my family, again.

Figure 14 Leroy and me in 2019

SECRETLY MARRIED AND REPERCUSSIONS

Leroy and I were careful not to be too open with our relationship. We were private people working in the very public field of journalism. As a woman, I didn't want anyone to think any less of me and my ability to perform the job. So we came and went according to our assignments. At one time, we worked in the same department for different stations. Imagine the day that we ended up on the same story! He was with WNBC, and I was with WCBS, and we had no idea we'd be there together that day. I chuckle just thinking about it.

Most people in the industry thought I was Leroy's little sister. A couple of friends knew better. Everything was going well until I went in to pick up my check after an assignment. The assignment editor gave Leroy's check to me, too. When Leroy went by later to pick up his check, the editor said, "Oh! We gave it to your little sister." Leroy had a fit. "That's not my sister! That's my wife!" And just like that, our secret was out.

Things went downhill from there. Accusations of assumed nepotism swirled in the air. Then, the accusations of us making double money began to float through the ranks. Unlike today, it was frowned upon to have family members working in the same business from a corporate perspective. Now people hire and recommend their family members all the time. It was a tough time for us. I couldn't understand why it was such an issue. We were, in fact, doing the work, but they didn't see it like that. We found ourselves working harder to gain more opportunities. The television station didn't want us to work simultaneously. At that time in the film industry, many women, particularly white, stayed at home while their husbands worked. In our case, we were both making decent money. They were basically counting our money and making assumptions. There was gossip in the field, and people even began to chide me, saying I was rich. It was almost as though we were being punished multiple times, once for being Black, again for being talented, and once more for being married.

Figure 15 Leroy & me

CHOOSING JOURNALISM

When I decided to change my field, I considered many options, but journalism was my first choice. I went on a quest to find my training ground. I went to the School and College Information Bureau to find out about journalism schools. Unfortunately, the only school they could recommend was a four-year college that I could not afford in time or money. I began calling different newspapers in the New York area to ask if they had any training programs for Blacks. I also inquired about the qualifications I'd have to meet to enter the program and field. There were no such training programs in existence at that time. However, most of the professionals who I spoke with suggested I take as many college courses in journalism as I could. I was making plans to begin those classes in the coming fall when I read in the *New York Times* that the *Manhattan Tribune* was going to start a new school of journalism for Blacks and Hispanics. The program was set to be financially backed by a major foundation. I applied immediately! I was accepted and excited about the program starting in July, but the school never did get started.

After waiting six months, the publisher wrote me a letter stating that the foundation had changed its mind about funding the program.

Deep Breaths & Big Risks

Since the newspaper was a new publication and couldn't support a school alone, I asked the publisher if I could stay with the paper as a volunteer. He agreed to my staying with the clear understanding that I would be on my own because the paper did not have the money for a full staff. There would also be no one with spare time to teach me. Despite this handicap, I was able to contribute several articles with contribute several articles with my byline printed in the *Manhattan Tribune*. I also became the calendar of events editor.

Figure 16 My first press card

Jessie's Grapevine

I started my journalism work at the New York Courier, a small community paper based in Harlem. A few of my articles also ran in the *Amsterdam News*. I ran a column called Jessie's Grapevine. My column allowed me to write about people who were just breaking into the entertainment industry. Everything I wrote was positive; I didn't write anything negative about anybody. I just did profiles. Some of the people I covered really were "it" and went on to do some big things. There was an agent that called me up and said, "Jessie, we got a new one. We want you to do a story on her. Her name is Melba Moore, and she's gonna be good!"

Melba was a great singer and a hit in *Purlie!* I also covered her then-boyfriend, Clifton Davis. I was the first one to do an article on Sherman Hemsley from Amen and The Jeffersons. Other notable stories in Jessie's Grapevine included coverage of Anna Maria Horsford, Isaac Hayes, and Woodie King.

Figure 17 Jessie's Grapevine article

When I left bacteriology, I wanted a job where I could be near the people. I didn't like being closed in too much. Starting out at the newspaper fulfilled some of that desire. I did like that I could do my work from anywhere and just send it in to the newspaper, but I didn't like the newspaper overall.

Jessie Maple

BROADCAST JOURNALISM

I was interested in journalism as a whole, but I was more intrigued by broadcast journalism. Broadcasted press reaches more people than any other news source in the world. It supports the notion that people are more influenced by what they see and hear compared to just reading.

The broadcast press also gives the person a chance to interpret a story as he sees it without having the story blue-penciled and edited out, as it is, in many cases, in printed journalism. You cannot edit out an inflection or tone of voice.

When I began my pursuit of journalism, our cities were changing rapidly, but the broadcast press changed very little. The demand for Blacks in every field of journalism was growing fast. As our cities grew Blacker and Blacker, after being deserted by whites, the need for Black journalists increased.

As Blacks became more aware of what was going on around them, their interest in Blackness increased, producing a strong desire and need to be well-informed. When we see and hear news from other Blacks, it is more readily accepted. We feel we are a part of what is happening.

I understood the power of broadcast journalism and foresaw the need for Black audiences to be reached en masse. Before I left the lab, Dr. King had been assassinated. That was a big mess, among other things. The racial tension continued to increase. Cities were becoming dependent on its Black radio and television news reporters to stop rumors and cool tensions. I recognized, then, how politicians would come to depend on the Black journalists and moderators to interpret their views to the Black constituency.

I chose a career in broadcast journalism as the best method to help my brothers and sisters, Black or white, to understand both sides of a story and be knowledgeable. During the beginning of my career, it was easy for people to be short on tolerance and long on prejudice and hate. A shortage of minority reporters to interpret the daily life of the inner city was causing the press to deliver news from its white viewpoint. The outcome was that Black and Latino news was delivered through the narrow lens of the extremes of human behavior. Hundreds of thousands of people were humiliated, intimidated, victimized by police brutality, subjected to consumer frauds, and exposed to callous and cynical indifferences. The Black stories weren't being told until the medical world or social agencies were ready to make a study of the "Negro problem" or when there was a riot or a scream on the street corner.

I felt that many of the white reporters were afraid to come to the communities and be among Blacks. If a reporter did not come into the communities to ask questions and see for themselves what was going on, how could they report the news accurately? Likewise, many Blacks would not talk to a white reporter because they felt as though they could not relate to the problem and, therefore, would write a one-sided story.

Jessie Maple

In 2019, I looked back at an old essay that I'd written to make sure I had gotten all my "whys" in place for choosing journalism. How interesting it is that my why in the seventies continues to be what pushes me now, nearly fifty years later? Many of the subjects that I was covering in the seventies and eighties are still relevant. We are still facing some of the same issues. The films I made may have been ahead of their time. It seems they could be of some use today!

THE APPRENTICE

Apprenticeships are a phase of working directly in the industry. You have an opportunity to work under the mentorship of someone that holds the role you are hoping to obtain. I tried everything I could to maximize my apprenticeships. My apprenticeship was focused on editing.

Work & Pay

During my time in the editing union, I worked on a film with an executive producer who wanted to use his own team from California. The editing union didn't want him to bring his team, but he brought them anyway. To try to fix things from his side, he was going to take away the apprenticeship. It wasn't written in stone, but they were just accommodating each other. Well, I was the apprentice on the film. I said, "No, you can't take away my job. I was promised this job, so you can't take it away."

"Oh, yes, I can," he emphatically replied.

I ended up taking him to court in Harlem. He hated that! Court in Harlem? He was out of his element! In an effort to appease me, he said, "We'll just pay you for the amount of time that you were going to work." Unfortunately, that wasn't what I wanted. I was an apprentice who desired hands-on experience. I said, "No, I want to work, and then I want to be paid."

I was able to get my just payment and the experience. That's the kind of person I am. I didn't let them treat me any kind of way. I had my coffee shop and could go serve the community and be treated wonderfully. I could also go back to the lab any time I wanted. Neither of those options was what I was interested in pursuing. They couldn't do anything to me. I always did what was right.

Reality Before Reality

I was an apprentice on the first gay television series. It was called *An American Family (1971)*. It featured this guy named Lance portraying his gay lifestyle, how his family accepted him and what they thought about it. He would dress up as a female. In fact, he was the first continuous portrayal of an openly gay, cross-dressing character on television. The show also focused heavily on the tensions that ultimately led to the family's breakup. Since then, the documentary series has been acknowledged as one of the first reality television shows.

Western Union Will Get Their Attention

Another one of my apprenticeship opportunities was under *The Harry Reasoner Report* on ABC. During my training, there were no other Blacks in the department. The head of the department had to walk me in. They told me later that meant that nobody had better have said anything to me. I worked in that department where people would send in short stories to be edited. But I didn't like some of the people in the department because they had attitudes. I didn't stay there long. I wanted to quit, but I felt so bad because of the man who had walked me in. It was expected that, since I was his pick, I would stay there until he said differently.

After about six weeks, I decided that I really couldn't stay there with that group of people. I didn't know how to leave, but I didn't want to go in. Over the next weekend, I wanted him to get the message before he checked on me on Monday morning. At that time, if you wanted to get someone's attention, you had to really do something big. Well, I decided to send my message that I wasn't returning through Western Union. Someone from the department saw me later and said, "We thought all of us were going to lose our jobs when that man came in showing us the Western Union!" That was the end of that.

CHOOSING THE UNION

When I left the lab, I spent a lot of time volunteering. I also began researching the kind of jobs that I could get in journalism with a particular focus on those that paid the most. The highest-paying jobs were in the union behind the camera. I said to myself, "Oh, boy, that's where I'm going!" I was in the editing union first, the 771 local union. People would inquire, "How did you do that?" I'd tell them I just went down there. Each time I'd go, they'd tell me, "We ain't got no jobs!"

I'd keep on walking right past whomever was saying it and proceed to ask as many questions as I wanted. "We only have jobs for our people," was a reply I received quite often. But none of that turned me around. The only time I cried was when I needed money to finish my film and wasn't getting it fast enough. I would cry for that, but all the general rejections didn't make me cry.

The Union Test

Taking the union test to become a camerawoman was the biggest challenge that I faced in my career. To pass the test you had to know the parts, features, and how to use the 16 millimeter and 35 millimeter cameras.

The Maple Crew

Every free moment I had, I was visiting the camera houses, looking at equipment, taking cameras apart, putting them back together, and running through each camera's unique features. Taking the time to learn this knowledge consumed me.

When it came time for my test, I had a group of, at least, six men standing around watching me, hoping that I would make a mistake. I went through the test with confidence, even doing some things perfectly that I hadn't been able to conquer previously. Once the test was over, they said I had made a mistake on the camera I knew the best, the 16mm Aeroflex. I was so disappointed. My sister Peggy and I cried and cried and cried! I had wanted to pass so badly. I wanted my family to be proud of me. That was the hardest thing for me.

Thankfully, Leroy had requested to be present for my test. He noticed a tester tampering with the camera that the report indicated that I'd failed. Upon meeting with the board of directors, I was given another test, the same day of the meeting, with no advance preparation. This time, with ten people present, including attorneys, and Leroy being barred from the room, I passed! I went through the equipment so quickly and without error that people were both shocked and embarrassed.

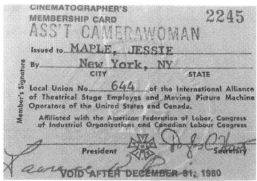

Figure 18 My union card

Jessie Maple

THE TRIAL PERIOD

Upon reopening my case, it was found that I, indeed, had been the subject of discriminatory practices. I was granted a six-week trial period with WCBS's local news! While there was excitement, I knew that it wasn't going to be easy. In addition to a rigorous review process at the end of each working day, a stenographer was to be present at each meeting, just in case there was a problem later on. The daily critiques included an assessment of my work with the assistant editor, the editor, the senior news manager, the assistant news manager, and many other odd people. The meetings were awkward, to say the least. I had hoped that would be the only thing that I had to endure during my trial period, but it wasn't. I dealt with crew members that didn't want to work with me. They felt as though being on my crew would not get them access to the glamorous stories but rather to the leftovers. There were whispers behind my back, conveniently audible enough for me to hear, about their disappointment in being assigned to my crew. On some sets, I noticed that, during breaks, no one was around; I never realized or thought to ask about a separate break area for crew members. Nevertheless, I persisted.

QUEASY HELICOPTERS AND OTHER SECRETS

I had a lot of secrets behind my success. Most of the mistakes and issues wouldn't have been a big deal for anyone else, but because I was a Black woman and had called out the unfair industry practices, I had to be as close to perfect as possible, although there is no true perfection. I had to be twice as good as the best guy. Fortunately, there were some things working in my favor that allowed me to keep my shortcomings under wraps. Every time I went out, I had to get the story. It didn't matter what the other part of the crew had to do. I had to get the story because it was all on me.

Queasy Helicopters

My punishment when I first started was to send me up in the helicopter. Every time they sent me up, I would get so sick that, sometimes, I had to hang out the window. Once I got the story, when we landed, Ronnie, the crew's electrician, would have to take me and help me stand up against a wall to get settled. I'd get so woozy that I couldn't stand up by myself. Ronnie would have to help steady me after each shoot.

One day, the girl at the assignment desk asked me how I was doing. I told her that I'd gotten sick, but I still got the story. She told me to go to the drugstore and purchase some over-the-counter motion sickness pills. "Take one of them," she said, and I did. I was great then, boy! With that, I would go up in the helicopter, at least, twice a day. Each time I went, it was sixty dollars, added to my pay, each trip. Once they saw that I got through that, then the other camera people wanted to take that away from me. I said, "Oh, no. This is my assignment. I want it every day." Sixty dollars each trip, two times a day! I was making a bunch of money!

Getting the Cold Scoop on Poop

When New York first made it a law to pick up poop after your dog, I was assigned to cover that story. It was one of the coldest days of the year, and I was headed to Central Park to get the story. It was so cold my hands froze, and I started to cry. The tears were just falling, but of course, I got the story. I always made it through the story. After I got the story, the reporter said, "Well, if you were cold, we would've come inside."

I said, "Yeah, right!"

If we had done that, they would have had a reason to get rid of me. They would have said I wouldn't have gotten the story.

Running from the Pope

I was assigned the story covering Pope John Paul II's visit to New York. Our crew was perched in a van, ready for action, when, all of a sudden, there was a tremendous ruckus at the door. It sounded like the thunder had arrived right at our doorstep with no respect for those of us inside. Imagine my surprise to find men in suits being the culprit of the heart-quickening storm of noise. Scared little me took off running in the other direction. Ronnie explained it was the FBI, demonstrating their ability to shake things up, if need be, as they canvased the area for safety. I'd never encountered that level of security for anything in my life. Once Ronnie convinced me to get back to my post, we were able to grab our story with no one being the wiser about my little sprinting snafu.

Everyone is capable of mistakes. Within a new environment or an entirely new career altogether, a steep learning curve is expected. However, the position I was in didn't allow me the luxury of beginners' errors. Instead, I was grateful to have a team that had my back. They covered for me, knowing that any slight infraction could mean the end of my dream before it really even came true.

Cat Nibbles and Comb-Overs

I shared that each story during my six-week trial period required a thorough review of my footage. The team would gather around the table with a mini television in view. Their purpose was to critique my camera work and identify any out-of-focus frames, wobbling shots, and any other idiosyncrasies they could find. They were not going easy on me, and I was usually prepared with my rebuttals. I remember two occasions that left a different energy in the room.

Cat Nibbles

I was shooting a story in which the reporter wanted to include the interviewee's pet cat in the story. Turns out the only way that the cat would cooperate was by nibbling on the woman's ear. Yes, you read that correctly. It took everything in me to keep my stomach settled from the disgust of that moment. I mean, the woman did the entire interview with a straight face while that cat sucked on her ear!

When I walked into the review room, the panel looked stunned. For the first time, there was a bit of silence before they dived in, saying, "Jessie! You shot the entire story with that cat nibbling on her ear! Is this some sort of joke?"

I shared with them that I wished it was a joke, but unfortunately, it was the only way to get the cat to participate in the shoot. I laughed as I explained the predicament that the knots in my stomach nearly put me in. They couldn't blame me for not getting the story that day!

Bald Spots & Comb-Overs

Another of my footage reviews brought me into the room to find all the men rubbing their heads. I don't know if I'd noticed before that day that they were all balding on the top. No one said a word while their eyes were glued to the screen. No doubt, they were staring in bewildered disbelief at the serious reporter as the four hairs on his head bent back and forth under the weight of the windy day. Ordinarily, these strands were meticulously smoothed into a forlorn comb-over. If those few hairs flapping in the wind were a distraction to me, I knew they would be to the audience, too! Couldn't he feel them tickling over head? I couldn't figure out how he managed to keep a straight face with all the movement going on. I'd asked the reporter numerous times if he wanted to pause so that he could adjust his coif. After multiple failed attempts and rising frustration, he demanded, "Just shoot it!" And that's exactly what I did. You know I wasn't going to argue with him. I wasn't going back without the story. The panel accepted my explanation of the day's events just before bursting into laughter.

I Made the Evening News

My footage reviews came with a lot of critiques. On one particular occasion, they made notes on the shakiness of my coverage. Everyone seemed to believe that I was proving them right, that I was fighting this battle for nothing. I certainly wasn't going to admit that I had terrible motion sickness and that they should be glad that I'd returned with any coverage at all. I offered my perspective on how the "moving" footage would provide the audience with the opportunity to feel as if they were in the boat with the crew. When I left, I wasn't sure that they'd bought it.

Later that evening, while I was watching the evening news with Leroy and Audrey, I discovered that my footage hadn't landed on the cutting room floor! There it was, inserted in the daily rundown of stories. I couldn't hide my excitement as we hooped and hollered all over the living room that day. Their usage of my film meant that I was on my way!

BIG STORIES

After my six-week trial period was over, they looked over my film work and decided that I could do the job. I went to work as a camerawoman for WCBS Local News. They put me on the freelance list and sent out a letter to the main working freelancers saying they couldn't just hire them anymore. "We've got to share the freelance work with Jessie Maple," they were told. Of course, they were mad. Many people thought I'd taken their jobs.

The way it worked was the assignment editor would call these certain two workers first, giving them first right of refusal. Then, they'd go on down the list. I was at the bottom of the list but was able to move to the top based on my work ethic and performance. Within about two weeks, I went from being a bottom cameraperson to the one that got called first. Me! I became the person they called first, the first person to get the job! My work helped me become the top cameraperson for the station!

I did not think that I'd be number one, but I knew that I knew my job and had proved it. By then, the reporters would ask for me. They would ask me to go out with them; whereas before, nobody wanted to work with me. The turning point came because I was good. I brought good stories and enough footage. I was never stingy and always gave the editors more than enough footage to work with, and they appreciated that. Jump cuts were not accepted at that time. They needed smooth transitions to get to another scene, so I gave them that. I even learned how to shoot to make sure that Black people were in the frames. Back then, Black people would be at the live coverage, but they'd end up on the cutting room floor. I learned how to shoot in a way that prevented them from being cut out, so the editors had to use them. Ronnie knew what I was doing, so he'd help me set it up to make sure that I was getting Black people in the story.

At that time, everything was still being done on film. There was this ridiculous belief that people of color and women couldn't shoot film, as if only white men possessed some special technique. I learned and made sure to do my job and do it well.

When I first started, I got all the cold stories, helicopter shots, and any others that were difficult. If the other two stations had the footage, I couldn't go back and say, "I didn't get it." They would try to say that I didn't get it because I was a woman. Some of the reporters would even try to play that trick and say, "I'm not going out there." But I knew all the games. I knew that, when we got back and if I didn't have a story, they'd say that I was a woman and they were afraid that I would get hurt. That's what happened with the milk strike.

Between Horses and a Wall (1979)

One of the biggest stories that I covered was the milk strike. The milk workers had gone on strike, and my crew and crews from the other stations were standing around, waiting. The milk strikers were up against a wall, and the police were on horses, standing in front of the strikers. I knew that they were going to break soon. The tension was so thick that someone was going to. The strikers were literally backed against a wall, and the heavy mounted police presence indicated they were anticipating something to break out, too. Many people felt that particular story was too dangerous for me. Even the reporter that I was with got scared. He tried to hold me back. But I knew, if I went back to the station without a story, I'd have been in trouble, especially if the other stations got it, so I basically beat him off me.

Let me explain. It was an extremely competitive industry at that time. My husband, Leroy, had taught me how to use the camera to my advantage. He told me, if anyone tried to hold me back or get me out of the way, to beat them with the camera. I was instructed to go from side-to-side and let the magazine hit them in the head.

The reporter was adamant. "I'm not going to get myself killed." I had Monica Smith, my soundperson, working with me. (To my knowledge, she was the first Black female sound technician in the union.) I said, "Look. Stay very close to me. When I move, you stick right with me."

She said, "Okay," and we moved.

Just as I got the reporter off me, they broke. I was able to get in between the horses and the people that were picketing and got a beautiful story. When we got back, the reporter came running down the steps, saying, "We got a letter from the head of the department saying what a beautiful story and footage we got!" Now he was standing on the sidelines; Monica and I were out there with the horses! You can laugh and roll your eyes. I always chuckle when I think about that part. But again, I think this is the perfect example of my determination and commitment to my work. I literally had to fight with the camera that day to get my story, but I didn't go back empty-handed.

New Jersey Chemical Waste (1979)

I received another commendation letter for doing a story on the chemical waste in New Jersey. I don't think it was a popular story that people wanted to cover. However, that's not why they sent me to cover it. They sent me out because I was good, and they knew that I'd bring them good footage. One particular news anchor asked for me after hearing that I had brought enough footage for the editors. I had moved up on their list from being no good to good – SHOCKER! The news caster wasn't friendly, but he asked for me to be the camera person on this story. I felt good because he wasn't a smiley person and he chose me. He was dry, but he knew what he needed to get the desired outcome.

Rockefeller (1979)

One of the stories that I remember well was when Rockefeller died. Because I was the top cameraperson, they called me first. Since it was late at night, it was an added bonus that I lived right in the city, on Fifth Avenue, and could get there quickly. However, I didn't want to go; I wanted to finish shooting my film. I was already preparing myself for going independent. There was a female assignment editor that said, "Oh, come on, Jessie, and just do this story for us." It was funny that they sent us because I knew that the woman that they claimed was with him in the townhouse when he died would not be there. We had to hide in the car for, at least, three days, waiting for her to come out. We were like spies at that time, but she never did come out because she was long gone. She had left before any of the news crews had gotten there. But I still did the story. That story would be one of my last news stories. It was as though there was an overnight switch to video.

IN ALL THE FRAMES

It was no big secret that many in the industry did not appreciate me being there. As a Black woman, I was an unwelcomed threat in an already highly competitive environment. In the beginning cameramen from different stations would form a tight, impenetrable band with their tripods. There would be no space for me. I looked at the situation and decided what I needed to do. I took my camera off the tripod and went portable. When the subject was announced, I heard someone say, "Oh, they're coming!" I ran right in the circle, placing myself smack dab in front of the camera people. Nobody could get a good shot because I was in all their frames!

They said, "Oh, she's crazy! Oh, she done lost her mind. She's in all our shots!"

But from that day on, they didn't try to block me out anymore, instead, they saved me a spot. I was bold and created my space like so many times before. The boldness isn't just for me. I want my people to know they are worthy of taking up space. Unfortunately, Black people have become accustomed to being invisible. They're hired help, or they're the lower-level worker. It doesn't matter. We all are worth fighting for our own space. If we don't, no one else will, and the circle will always block us from getting the beautiful shots of life.

Carry the Heavy Load

When I entered the news industry, there was this notion that women would not be able to carry the heavy camera equipment, but I made it work. There's a picture of me as a camera assistant carrying a heavy, awkward tripod while walking beside a strapping cameraman who had one free hand and one small camera in the other hand.

Looking at the picture, many people would probably wonder why it was that way. But that's the way of the business. I had to do my job just as well as any man.

Figure 19 Me carrying the camera

Leroy had taught me how to handle the equipment and had advised me to get everything at once when on assignment, so I didn't have to go back to the car and hold up the crew. Everyone on my crew knew that when we left the car, they needed to take everything in one trip because I was locking the door. Since I got all my equipment in one trip, there was no going back. That's what they would want, an excuse to point out a woman's inferiority compared to a man's strength. I wasn't going to be the woman to give it to them.

Figure 20 Me carrying the CP16 camera

It's a Man's World

> *This is a man's world, this is a man's world*
> *But it wouldn't be nothing, nothing without a woman or a girl*

I like the song "It's a Man's, Man's, Man's World" by James Brown particularly for his acknowledgement of women's contributions. Unfortunately, the two industries I chose to have careers in, medicine and film, are male dominated. They don't always welcome women or what we can bring to our professions. My efforts were never to put a man down. They were simply for women to experience equality, both in opportunity and compensation.

When I took my first video class, I used the lyrics to "It's a Man's, Man's, Man's World" to demonstrate what James Brown was singing about with pictures. The instructor and class loved it! They ended up using the video as a promotion for students to take the class.

No, I Need a Four

I had a lot of fun during my Maple Crew days in the mid to late seventies and early eighties. No, I didn't get any pinches and pats on the behind, especially since my husband Leroy worked in the industry, too. He was tall with strong muscles, and everybody knew him. Everyone knew, by now, we were married.

I was shooting one day, and we had a meter that we used to set the camera to determine how much light we wanted to come on the subject. A guy came on as relief for one of the people that didn't come to work that day. I told him, "I'd like a four."

He said, "You don't need a four. I'll give you what I want to give you."

I said, "No, I need a four."

And then Ronnie said, "You know who her husband is?"

And he replied, "Who? I don't care."

"You know that tall, big Black guy that works for WNBC?"

The light just lit up then! After the news got around about that, nobody really bothered me.

FUN IN THE SPOTLIGHT

I covered a lot of serious stories during my time in the news. However, there were a few times when I was working when I was able to really have a good time. I was especially thrilled when I got to make people's eyes go wide when I was doing my work. Two instances still make me smile when I think of them.

Do That Again, Sister

As long as I was working, I was able to take the car and credit card home over the weekend. One particular time, the assignment desk called me on the car phone while I was in Harlem, and I stopped in front of a group of brothers to take the call. The brothers said, "Sister, do that again for us." They said, "What is that?"

I explained to them that it was a car phone, and the assignment desk was calling me to do a story. At that time, there were no portable cell phones. Man! Those brothers started slapping fives, wanting me to do it one more time. "Pick up the phone one more time and talk!"

Showing Off with Lab Friends

There was a film shooting in Harlem where they didn't have a cameraman. I got to fill in and show off for my lab friends. They all came off their posts at work to see me work that big camera. That was a sight! I am sure they were thinking, little Jessie from the lab, who they knew to be doing all the research, was handling the big metal tripods and magazines! She said she was leaving and look at her now!

Figure 21 Me with camera

FROM NEWS TO FILM

Transitioning from the newsroom and editing floor to independent film was something that I knew I had to do. I knew that the industry was moving from film to video. People would ask me why I worked so much; I had to prepare myself to be ahead of the change. I knew that my work in film would be limited once they began advancing to video, which happened practically overnight. I needed income, so I worked all the shifts. I worked during the midday news, six o'clock evening news, and the eleven o'clock late news. I had to change crews. The first crew had been there for years and would say, "No, I'm not going to work overtime." I told them that they'd been working for twenty years, and I was just getting started.

I prepared myself because, when you're Black, you've got to have all the licenses. You can't go anywhere half-stepping. I got my first- class FCC license. We were told it was one of the requirements to shoot video. They'd promised the workers that had been at the station a long time that they were going to train them for a different union focused on video. None of that came true. The older guys retired. I was ready, if I chose, to go the way of video. I had my license and was in the union.

When they first came out with video, the camera was very heavy. At that point, I decided that I didn't want to go into another union or carry that equipment. My interest in writing had stayed with me from my newspaper days. I began creating stories that I turned into scripts. It was then that I decided to become an independent filmmaker. I wrote the stories, produced them, directed them, and raised the money. When you're the writer, director, and producer, it's your story. You own the rights to every part of the process.

Although I had my FCC license, I wasn't interested working in video. I joined a program that focused on film production. Everyone in the program had scripts they hoped to develop. Everyone worked on each other's projects. I wrote, directed and produced my first film, *Will,* about the drug epidemic that was plaguing the Harlem community.

While in the program, my film was selected to be submitted for a grant opportunity. At that time, *Will,* was in the production phase and was accepted. That's how I switched over from news to independent filmmaking.

GOOD MUSIC AND PRIVATE PARTIES

While I have maintained a demanding career, I like to have fun, too. I'm not big on going out, but I enjoy having a good time. I've never drank alcohol of any sorts or smoked cigarettes, so I find enjoyment in other ways. One of my favorite things to do is listen to the blues and dance. And by dance, I mean slow drag. It's nothing for me to have a private party with my imagination and good music. I'll put on some B.B. King, Z.Z. Hill or Esther Phillips records and pretend that my beau is there with me. I put my arms up like they are around his neck, and I sway to the rhythms, allowing myself to get carried away in the moment. Similarly, when I have parties, I slow drag with Leroy or dance around with friends.

Years ago, I would travel to California, so I could see Esther Phillips. I really enjoyed her music, and it became a tradition of mine. The Black night clubs in California had lots of beautiful Black people dressed to the nines. Men in hats sat around the bar. They were jamming to the music and talking trash. I'd be alone, sitting at the bar, drinking my non-alcoholic fruit punch. Esther would come down the stairs singing. It was exciting for us to just be in the place, having fun. The atmosphere was stacked with handsome men and women showing love to one another.

I also like Tina Turner. I get to be her each year at our family Christmas talent show. I grab a shawl with the fringes on it and just shake so they'll move!

Although I didn't go out much, when I did go out in New York, I'd go to local clubs to listen to music. Musicians tell stories, and I really like that. I introduced my grandson, Nigel, to blues music before he was six. He'd ask me, "Grandma, why do I like this kind of music?"

I'd tell him that it's in his soul like it's in mine. Music has changed in many ways over the years. Although different rhythms and styles have come about, it still connects with people. Even rap music tells stories. All good music tells a story.

I like feeling good. Cooking up fantasies, indulging in good music and enjoying my own company are ways that I can tap into a good mood. Regardless of what's going on in the outside world, I've found the ability to keep myself smiling.

PART 2:
GAINING MY INDEPENDENCE

Jessie Maple

FEATURE FILMS AND DOCUMENTARIES

Though I was part of the union with my television work, it was important for me to remain independent with my film work. Founding my own production company enabled me to produce the works I wanted to see. I could hire who we wanted. And ultimately, I maintained creative control over every project I embarked upon. Moreover, I was able to retain a larger share of profits by handling most of the work myself. Later, I expanded my service offerings to help other independent artists bring their visions to life and share them with audiences.

Independent feature films and documentaries have been the things that I have gained notoriety for. Writing a big Hollywood story has never been my dream. I didn't seek out sensational or trending topics to build on. Instead, when choosing to make a film, I write about things that bother me. The stories I tell are meaningful to me in one way or another. I've been privileged to shine a light on what some would consider to be dark places. I've been called crazy and told that no one would be interested in what I wanted to cover. I chose to shoot the stories that mattered to me anyway. I've had films, long and short, that have been celebrated from coast to coast and beyond. They were birthed from my imagination and experience. Through it all, one of the things that I'm most proud of is that all my films and documentaries were shot on location in Harlem.

Will (1981)

Will was my first full-length film. It starred a young Loretta Devine. She was fresh out of college. It was her first film. I wrote *Will* about something that bothered me, drug addiction. Because I believe you can always lift yourself up, I crafted a story of a family coming together in an uncanny way. The main character, Will, and his wife adopted a young boy, Lil Brother, who was headed toward the same drug-addicted lifestyle that Will was coming out of. I was able to tell the story of Will's battle with drug addiction and the saving of Lil Brother without explicit details being featured in the film.

Figure 22 On the set of Will with Loretta Devine

Figure 23 On the set of Will

Twice as Nice (1989)

In Twice as Nice, I cast two non-actors in the main roles. UCLA women's basketball stars Pamela and Paula McGee were at the center of the story. WNBA player and coach, Cynthia Cooper-Dyke, was also a part of the main cast.

The film focused on twin sisters that were competing to be part of the draft. In a way, the film was also a coming-of-age tale because the young ladies learned quite a bit about the real world as they went through their experiences. The film can also be considered ahead of its time, as it was shot years before the formation of the WNBA in 1996.

I shot most of the film on location in Harlem. We also used a college out in Long Island for some scenes. It kept with my theme of using the resources that were around me.

Figure 24 On the set of Twice as Nice

Methadone: Wonder Drug or Evil Spirit

One of our coffee shops was next to a methadone clinic. I was fascinated by the people and outraged by how they handled the addicts. They were coming in to get their methadone treatments, and the people in charge knew just the trick they were playing on them. The patients were stuck! What they said they were trying to do versus what they were actually doing to the people who were addicted to drugs weren't in sync. The people would come into our diner and have coffee before or after their treatments. I heard their stories and said, "I'm going to do a film about you all."

At that time, the documentary was considered too political and wasn't well received because I was challenging the notion that the treatment was helpful.

Black Economic Power: Reality or Fantasy (1977)

Black Economic Power: Reality or Fantasy was a documentary that I produced to look at economics within the Black community. Many critics labeled the film as too political; therefore, it didn't garner as much traction as it probably should have. The film featured Don King and basketball player Earl Monroe. Although the film was created more than thirty years ago, the concept is still relevant today. Are Blacks able to achieve and sustain economic power?

I've done many other projects in addition to these. My inspiration and approach remain the same. I want to tell the stories about things that bother me which may not otherwise be told. I strive to use the resources that are around me. Most importantly, I work to give voice to my people and the challenges we face.

My Process

Over the years, many people have inquired about my filmmaking process. It all begins with a story and outcome for me. I write scripts and give the characters their due focus. I usually move quickly from point A to point B. That's where I get into a situation – wanting to just get to the point. When I work with editors, they, sometimes, tease me about the fillers being absent. I just want to get to the main parts, but other people want all the details. For example, when I was working on my last book, *Keisha & Bobby*, there were a lot of additional details that needed to be included. I don't like spending a lot of time getting my characters to where they are going, but audiences enjoy that. Even in writing this book, I just wanted to tell the parts that made me happy. However, there is a journey on the way to the destination. I take a similar journey for each project: 1) Have an idea or goal, 2) Gather the resources, 3) Start (without waiting on other people's approval or input), and 4) Don't look back until it is done. This process continues to serve me well.

Budgets & Grants

As you may imagine, making films over thirty years ago was an expensive process. Much of the work on my productions was done in-kind. Would you believe that I produced Will for under $12,000?! A turning point in my ability to produce films came when I learned about grants. I was astounded that people were basically giving away money to get works done. All I needed was for someone to show me how to complete the proposal one time, and from there, I was off!

Grants and in-kind work made up a large portion of my production budgets. I worked with others in the industry to accomplish each task. Recently, grant funding has been instrumental in the preservation of my earlier works.

Women's Film Preservation Fund

While Will was recognized as the first full-length independent feature film, it did not reach a broad audience until much later. In 2015, the New York Women in Film and Television's Women's Film Preservation Fund restored the work. The film is now a part of their library.

National Film Preservation Fund

My film, *Twice as Nice*, was selected by the National Film Preservation Fund for restoration in 2015. As one of fifty-seven films chosen, the grant allowed my work to extend what its lifetime would have been, if it had been left untouched. The preservation process made my film available to larger audiences.

As I look back, I am glad these opportunities came along. The works deemed too political decades ago can now be accessed by the activists that continue the work today. A small budget back then can make a big impact now. I'd love to continue seeing the revival of my earlier work.

Too Political

I shared that a few of my films were considered too political. However, I really don't see myself as being political. I was merely telling my stories from my vantage point. I see myself as being a Black woman fighting for the rights of Black women. I never thought about the political realm. I didn't really know anything about being socially provocative. Outsiders made that delineation. They'd view my films and say, "That's too political. We can't show that." I wasn't attempting to be political. I was pointing out what I thought to be obvious occurrences.

In addition to the general politics narrative, I've heard that some circles include me in their Civil Rights accounts, concerning Blacks and women. That wasn't the initial goal. It was simply the outcome of my insistence on fairness as I worked to gain access to my fair due.

The Schomburg Center for Research in Black Culture, Harlem's research library, right where I was doing my work back then, didn't have any of my films. They said *Black Economic Power* and everything I was doing was too political. Now the Center has my first book, but still nothing more. The Museum of Modern Art (MOMA) on 53rd Street bought a copy of *Methadone: Wonder Drug or Evil Spirit*, purchased a copy of my book, and showed *Twice as Nice* almost two years ago.

The filmmakers that are out today are clear to make political works. Some of them are really pushing the boundaries and allowing us to see many firsts. I think, right now, there is a surge in the creation of politically charged films. However, in some cases, it is more about popularity and attention. I say this because so many people put out their work and opinions only to take it back at the first sign of challenge. I believe people should do the work because it is right, not because it's trendy.

20 West – Home of Black Cinema

One of our largest entrepreneurial undertakings was not one that I'd planned for. I needed a place to show my film that I'd just completed at the American Film Institute in California as a participant in the directing program. There was a still photography studio down the street from where I lived that had a small theater. I asked the owners to use the space to show my film. While they agreed, the conditions for usage were that I would have to show my film on the cleaning night. I went by to check it out on cleaning night; there were hoses and electric cords all over the floor. I said, "No! I can't do this. All my girlfriends have fur coats. They like to dress up and wear high-heel shoes." Our film showings were a big deal.

Figure 25 Leroy & me at 20 West

Leroy and I had a brownstone. I asked him if he thought we could get a little theater going in the basement within a month. His reply was, "Yeah, we can do that." So we opened up 20 West, Home of Black Cinema. And that's how the legendary 20 West got started.

Black independent film was an edgy concept. Looking back, it was quite fitting that we would choose the unconventional location of our basement after everything was said and done. We ended up creating a viewing space large enough to seat fifty. Our guests became our members, and we wanted them to feel at home. We made our own popcorn, and people bought their own pillows. This space was as much for them as it was for us. It was ours.

Things to Do in New York

Twenty West was listed in a "Must Do in New York" guide for visitors. We had audiences from all over the world, including Paris. Our intimate theater was similar to the theater houses there and other places abroad. We attracted people from all walks of life to our brownstone. They were all there to get their dose of independent films.

Figure 26 Bob Law

Bob Law

Bob Law was known to most as a radio host on WWRL. But to us and 20 West, he was an angel. He hosted a midnight show called, *Night Talk*. Bob carried the world on his shoulders. He allowed others to express their feelings on his show. He had a large audience and never hesitated to share the showings of 20 West with his listeners. In fact, when people were concerned about *The Color Purple* content, he suggested that they visit 20 West as an alternative. We were showing *Sugar Cane Alley* at the time. Everything we did relied on word of mouth and Black media outlets.

When we opened 20 West, people tried many things to discourage us, but we owned the building. There were a lot of things involved and to be considered when doing something of that magnitude. There was the rent and lights and so many other things to be mindful of. There were also people who weren't on board with Leroy and me because they thought we were doing too much. That's the only reason that I could think of for some of the feedback we received because we were really doing something positive.

We had a number of things going for us at 20 West. Both patrons and filmmakers benefited from our existence. People knew they could bring their kids without having to put a napkin over their eyes. We rented the films and brought the artists in town when we could. We didn't believe in doing anything for free because we knew first-hand how hard it was. We connected with some people in Westbury Village on Long Island to help filmmakers make more money. For example, if a filmmaker came from California, we'd set three showings to make their trip worthwhile. They'd come to 20 West for a showing. Then, they'd go to Westbury. They'd leave their stop in Westbury at a theater doing something similar with independent films. Next, they would go to Milwaukee for screenings. My dear friend Debra J. Robinson who was a professor at the University of Wisconsin – Milwaukee, would set up and host these events. Each time they went, they were speaking and getting paid. We had created our own tour circuit. We knew what life was like for independent filmmakers, so we made it a priority to have the money ready right away when they came. Debra would pick them up, have the check in hand, and take them straight to the bank! She'd do it before she even showed the film. We knew how it could be with us; since we were in a better position than the filmmakers we were inviting, we took care of business. We rented their films. We gave them what they needed – a place to show their films and the money to support their work. Our efforts extended to scores of young filmmakers. Debra and I are still good friends who continue to support each other's work to this day.

Haile Gerima is a film professor at Howard University. During the time that 20 West was thriving, he'd make recommendations and tip us off to the films we should be showing. He knew the up and comers on the independent film scene. Haile proved to be an invaluable resource in helping us curate the films for 20 West.

We showed the independent films of everyone that we knew or heard of. We even showed all of Spike Lee's earlier films up to and including *She's Gotta Have It*.

Figure 27 A 20 West season calendar

Things began to taper off as everyone began saving themselves for the big productions. Everyone had high hopes of being Hollywood's next big filmmaker.

I wasn't planning to stay at 20 West long. The plan was to stay there for a year or so until my film career took off. I ended up staying there for nine years because our audience wouldn't let us go. They loved the theater so much! They wanted me and Leroy to be there when they visited. Later, I would see some of the members, and I would feel bad. They'd say, "Jessie, you've got to come back. You and Leroy have to come back because we don't have a place to go to see independent films."

Pick It Up

We did not get paid for our work at 20 West. We were supported by grants and memberships, but there wasn't a salary in it for me or Leroy. Ultimately, I had taken up nine years of my filmmaking time to run 20 West. While it was nice, it wasn't what I wanted to be doing, especially since so many people were becoming more reluctant to be independent as they pursued their Hollywood dreams. I decided it was time to go. We had people who were interested, and I thought somebody would pick it up and say, "Well, I'm going to do this now." But no one ever did. We went back to pursuing our films, and that was the end of an era for 20 West.

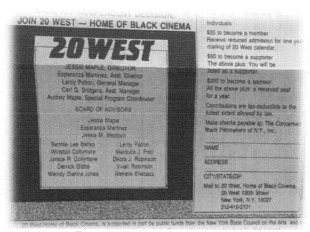

Figure 28 20 West membership form

MORE THAN MOVIES

I mentioned previously that we owned the brownstone where we housed 20 West. Our ownership was one of the things that made it possible for us to serve the community in many ways. Because we owned the brownstone, we had the freedom to fill it as we saw fit. Leroy and I had experienced more than our fair share of difficulties and disappointments. Because we knew the, sometimes, unwelcomed freelancer life, we took special care to make sure that we created a welcoming environment for them. We knew how hard it was to provide steady income proof and solidify references. So, when freelancers and musicians came looking for housing, we said yes.

We didn't check their references either. We just extended to them what we felt was fair – housing without judgement and obstacles. Our other tenants were homosexuals. At the time, there was still a large stigma about their lifestyle. Again, Leroy

Figure 29 Selling fruit outside of 20 West

and I had both experienced our own journeys with discrimination, so the least we could do was provide a safe home for them. Our home ended up being a welcoming place for the often-unwelcomed people. We were more than a brownstone. We were our own community. Yes, 20 West was home to Black cinema, but it was also a home for many within our community.

Jessie Maple

ON FRIENDSHIP

All productions require a solid crew, and I've been blessed to have an amazing support team at each step of my career. I want you to meet the Maple Crew, personal and professional.

My family members weren't the only good people in my life. I've met some wonderful people over the years. There have been some relationships that have really made an impact on me. I've lost contact with some friends, but the fondness of our interactions remains fresh in my memory. Others are still with me after more than twenty-five years of carrying on. Part of telling my story involves acknowledging them and the impact they've had on my life, personally and professionally.

Dressing Up with Delmar Thomas

While working on a couple of feature films with this difficult editor, I met my good friend, Delmar Thomas, during one of these assignments. Even though we were apprentices, the more senior team members didn't want us to work with the film. They wanted us to be their coffee girl and boy. We'd be dressed up, even though we were just apprentices. I wore long dresses as part of my style, and Delmar had a keen fashion sense of his own. We dressed fabulously every day and would be the sharpest people on the film set. The 1940s long dresses became my signature look. Although I don't see

Delmar often, he remembers how much I liked wearing long dresses. He says he thinks about me whenever he sees someone in a long, fabulous dress.

Figure 30 Me in one of my long dresses

Carol Morton

When I first started out, Carol was already working for Channel 13 WNET. I was just applying to the film program. She said, if I didn't get in,

Figure 31 Carol and me at her house31

Figure 32 Carol and me at American Film Institute

she would give up her spot in the program because she was already working in the industry. Carol was a producer and a writer. She would babysit for me sometimes. We were good friends. She, like some of my other friends at that time, were interested in Leroy's work. He was a still photographer, and his Jet centerfold photos, in particular, had garnered him a lot of attention. In fact, she's the one that discovered that Leroy was married and called me up and told me about it. It wasn't uncommon to come across Carol and me in the same spaces. She would share her information with me. We were friends and colleagues working together to get ahead.

Carl Bridgers

For a couple of summers in the early eighties, I was the Black Film Festival Director at Syracuse University. It all started with Audrey convincing one of her professors to bring me up to share a film. When he realized that I was working at the level I was, not just a family videographer a student was bragging on, it was on! I didn't just take my

Figure 33 Carl Bridgers

work; I brought Spike Lee's films, Carlos Diegues' *Quilombo* and other films that we were showing at 20 West during my visits. One particular time, I was delivering my message on the benefits of independent ownership, but that's not what the young people wanted to hear. They were more interested in how I got into film, what it would take to get to Hollywood. I indulged in a bit of the conversation, but afterward, one young man seemed to have really taken my initial information to heart. His name was Carl Bridgers, and he approached me after the program with his resume in hand. From that moment, it just worked having him in our world.

After graduation, Carl worked as a graphic artist at Fox News in New York City. He volunteered his design skills to 20 West, handling our graphics and publications. Carl also designed our graphics for 20 West's end of the year fundraiser. During that time, I'd push, and Carl would say, "You know I don't have to do this. I do have a full-time job," but he'd pick up the pace, and we'd laugh and keep going. He was so committed to us and 20 West that he ended up moving into the brownstone we owned next door. He became a part of our family. Since then, Carl has grown up and has a family of his own.

Carl and I don't see each other much these days. However, when our paths do cross, there's always a big hug in store for us both. He'll send me cards when something comes my way. He, like others, probably thinks I've forgotten about them, but I haven't. They'll always be close to my heart.

Ronnie

Getting my feet into the union was tough, and when I finally got there, everyone wasn't so eager to work with me. They weren't sure how I would be. During my WCBS trial, I was introduced to my dear friend Ronnie. He made up the third member of our three-man crew. He was the electrician.

Ronnie stuck with me and had my back. He was often the driver, especially on really long trips. He was a friend that helped me get my bearings together when things got a little mixed up on some of my assignments. Our friendship was fast and deep. Together with him and Monica Smith, our sound person, we made up the Maple Crew. When we were together, we had so much fun that people used to call us "Ronnie and the Supremes." I still chuckle when I think about how many of our daily work adventures unfolded. Because Ronnie was around me so much, he really knew me. He knew how I operated. He didn't take my presence as a threat. Instead, Ronnie understood the necessity for me to be successful. He never tried to minimize or take that away from me. In fact, he helped others fall in line when they worked with our crew. There was a mutual level of respect, and for that, I'm grateful. I'm blessed to have had our paths cross at such a critical point in my career.

Esperanza "Candy" Martinez

I've always valued the gift of friendship. In the early eighties, when 20 West was really thriving, Candy was my backbone. She had her full-time job with ABC's news department as director of news, yet managed to still find time to volunteer at 20 West as the assistant director and membership coordinator. Candy really believed in our vision and demonstrated her support by working tirelessly to ensure that everything was done correctly. Her primary role at 20 West was to manage membership, and, boy, was she good at it! She kept the records up-to-date for who was a member and where they were in terms of their membership dues. Candy didn't just stop with the dues of what we had, she went after those that she was connected to at work and other places to get them to become members. One of the running jokes was that members that she worked with would try to duck her for annual dues, but never quite escaped because she knew their pay schedules. Candy would catch them at the office and have them pay right then. She made the job of dues collection look easy. In addition to dues, Candy was responsible for writing the newsletters each month. She made sure that our members knew what the happenings were regarding 20 West.

One of the things that I marvel at, regarding Candy, was her loyalty. She was extremely faithful to me. She knew that, when I said something, I was going to do it. Beyond that, I think that faithfulness was part of her nature all along, and it benefited me and 20 West tremendously.

When I made the decision to close 20 West, I was anxious and tired. There was so much pressure during the transition that I completely forgot to tell Candy. about a year later, when I saw her, with intense eyes, she asked, "Jessie, why didn't you tell me? Why didn't you tell me you were closing?" It was hard to believe that I was so swept up in everything else that I neglected to tell one of the main people involved with 20 West what I was doing. It hurt me to see her hurt. I've since apologized, and we're still friends. She doesn't like talking on the phone as much, but when we see each other, not much is lost. She even celebrated with me at the Lincoln Center during my recognition a few years back.

Debra J. Robinson

While some of the relationships of my life have changed over the years, my friendship with Debra has remained as strong as ever. When I was working on my film, *Twice is Nice*, she found out that I had been working on it but still had a ways to go, particularly with the editing process. She called me and told me to stop talking, put the film in a box, and get it to her in Milwaukee. Debra had just gotten a new Steenbeck editing machine which would make the process significantly easier and faster. She edited the film, and I just stayed around until it was finished. Later, she invited me to be a guest lecturer in the film department at the University of Wisconsin – Milwaukee.

During that summer, we became tight. It just seemed to work. We were so tight that when she decided to move to Atlanta, I was one of the first people she reached out to.

Later, when Debra was working on a film in Ohio, I was able to return the favor by going to lend a hand. Over the years, she has edited several projects, feature films, shorts and documentaries. Her name comes up a lot on my projects.

During a speaking engagement at the Brooklyn Film Academy, it was noted that we were the only independent filmmakers who seemed to work on each other's projects. We were a mutual help to one another. Because we knew there was enough room for both of us to succeed, it wasn't a competition.

Debra lives in Atlanta now, and we remain dear friends. We continue to support each other's projects. While she still works on her projects, she's giving back to the next generation as a high school video teacher.

ON FANTASIES AND GOOD TIMES

Not only do I have good relationships in real life, I've built strong connections with some of the characters I've created through fantasies. After experiencing so much rejection and opposition, most people would have quit or been crushed attempting to sustain the lifestyle I was living. But I had a special gift — imagination. I used my imagination to create fantasies as an escape. Through fantasizing I could envision and enjoy endings as I saw fit.

Many, but not all, of my fantasies are inspired by people in my life. I take the admirable elements and, sometimes, the most prominent flaws, and put them in the pot for creating the characters that I do life with. I am able to hyper-focus on the qualities that stand out to me the most about individuals. I can exaggerate their characteristics – good and bad - to drive a particular outcome. Their presence allows me to process difficult situations, and their presence offers me a chance to live in someone else's life. And then there are times that my mind just wanders, and I meet interesting people along the way. A couple of fantasy characters that I've connected with have stayed with me, like those of Jake and Gigi. They've been with me so long in my fantasies that I think it is only fair that you get to meet them. They're part of the Maple Crew, too. Some elements of their fictitious existence allowed me to process some of the other scenes in my life.

Fantasy: Jake

As you can imagine and have probably guessed by now, relationships were tough to come by for a woman like me. I was considered too independent for the time. The men in the industry considered me intimidating. My first husband deemed me too ambitious. My current husband, however, decided that it was easier to climb with me. I explored different characteristics in my stories. I used my creativity to create a charismatic character named Jake. He represented all the elements that seemed to escape my grasp in many ways. He was passionate, yet sensitive. Jake was a real cool cat – a lover boy. He was cool and very sophisticated. It was fun to build his interactions.

Fantasy: Gigi

Another of my favorite characters is Gigi. She's based off my sister, Peggy, who was a nurse. In my collections, Gigi is a doctor. However, she realizes she's unhappy practicing medicine in the United States. She makes a bold choice to leave the States and head to Africa to pursue her dreams and true happiness. I like to think that, when she left, she found herself better for the choice.

I mention Jake and Gigi specifically because I have such a strong connection with them. While I always try to make my characters believable, there is a joy in being able to take on risks and experiences that I might not experience myself. I can control their destinies, and their endings are always sweet and joyful.

PART 3:
LESSONS AND HIGHLIGHTS

Jessie Maple

MAPLE CREW VALUES

In interviews, I am often asked how I got to where I am and how I've stayed so long. My answer is simple – consistency. My consistency in character is something that I've carried with me all my life. Many of the values that I hold dear are the ones that were instilled in me by my mother and father. I am convinced that staying true to these values is what has kept me going for so long.

Fearlessness

I had no fear back when I was in the lab and first starting in film work. If people talked to me crazy, I'd talk back to them crazy. Some of it I was able to capture in fantasies if I really wanted to go off. My fearlessness has always been with me. I was born in Mississippi and thought that no one could talk me down or put me down. I'm glad that my mother got me out of there because I don't know what would have happened to me if I'd stayed. I knew, whatever I did, I had to be good. You can't talk back unless you have no fear and know what you're doing! That's what kept me from getting fired.

Goodness

Goodness is also among my most prominent characteristics. I try to be good to people, no matter who they are. I never saw my father and mother being mean to anyone. There was plenty of meanness going on, but I've been treated good through my struggles. I try to pass that on.

I've never liked the term "boss," so when I work with people, we all are working together to create something. Therefore, we are all humans and equals. I try to treat people accordingly. I compensate people fairly for their time. I support others in the pursuit of their goals in whatever ways I am able. That can be time, resources, money or other things. I am a giver by nature, so I do it all with the same level of goodness.

There's also something to be said for doing things beyond self. The work that I did often came from a selfless place. In all that I did, my goal was to make it better for the next. That generosity is reciprocated. I had some good people around me who helped me make it happen. Goodness begets goodness.

Faith - I Believe

You're going to get many disappointments in life, but you'll get through it. No matter how low in life you get, you can bring yourself up. But you have to do it yourself, and then other people will help you and follow you through those crises. I share this message of faith a lot in my work. You can be what you want to be. I believe it. That's even how I sign my books now with "I believe."

Discipline

Discipline has been another important value in how I built my credibility. From studying the cameras for my union test to creating my own film, it has taken discipline to gain and maintain respect. Audrey was on the set with me once and said, "Mommy, you don't act like Mommy." I was just that disciplined that, even with my daughter on the set, I was consistently focused and professional. When you're responsible for a project, if you don't take charge and keep things in order, someone else will. They'll take over, and you'll find yourself doing what they say to do. I believe in being disciplined by not being mean, even though I mean business.

Training & Education

In addition to my other values, I believe that most of the things we need can be accessed through learning. There's some sort of program out there for each thing that we need to do. For instance, when I went into the medical field, I went to school for medical technology right after high school graduation. The school was called The Franklin School of Science & Art, and students came from around the world to attend. I took the course, passed the necessary test for working in the lab, and got a job. That same pattern followed me when I changed careers. When I was transitioning into film, I found programs that would allow me to work and train simultaneously with Channel 13 News and Third World Cinema. I spent about two years in film school for editing. I tell these stories to others, so they can keep moving forward. With the right training and education, you can even begin again.

Figure 34 Me as a student at Franklin

Figure 35 My professors and class at Franklin

Independence

I mentioned before that when I was coming up in the film industry, many people were saving themselves for Hollywood. I never had those dreams. I believed that we could all be successful independently within our own communities. If we had all stayed independent and worked collaboratively, imagine how far we would be by now.

I've had the opportunity, many times over the years, to go mainstream. I have chosen not to. Thus far, I haven't had an offer that I believe worthy of me giving up everything. It may take me a little longer to get things done, but I get them done. There's also that part of me that does not like to wait on other people. By the time they give their nod of approval or their contribution, I'm usually already on to the next thing. By remaining independent, I've been able to stay true to my core values, control my timeline on things, and help the people in my community in meaningful ways. Some things you just can't put a paid value on.

Work Ethic

In high school, I had a classmate who was the class president and smartest girl in the school. She was a beautiful person. One day, shortly after high school, I was in the subway in Philadelphia. I saw her, and she ran from me. She told me not to touch her because she was a prostitute and didn't want me to get the disease. She was one of the most beautiful people I'd ever met, so it was hard for me to see her in that state. Maybe she didn't have the options for making money. I always had something else to do, some way to make money and stay out of trouble. I sold Avon; I was a short-order cook. To this day, I'm not afraid to work. People will say, "Didn't I just see your movie? And now you're selling cookies?" I'd say, "Yeah, that was me last night, and right now, I'm selling cookies."

I'm not a person that does just one thing at a time. I have a bunch of activities taking place simultaneously because I can get it all done. Some people tell me just do one thing at a time, but that's just not me. I really do enjoy working.

The Maple Crew

Figure 36: Me as a short order cook

During my news broadcast years, I probably worked more overtime hours than most people in the industry at the time. Not only did I work in news for the first shift, I picked up additional shifts to earn extra money. My weekends were spent working on my films. In the midst of all of that, I was also enrolled in various training programs to hone my craft. I think that's a message to the young people — you can get what you want; it just requires work. I still work now, but not nearly as much as I used to. My husband still goes to work in the industry every day – by choice. I think young people can accept the messaging that working hard early on and maintaining independence can be the foundation for a liberated future.

It's All in Reach

I have a strong notion that everything we need is in reach. It's with this philosophy that I made intentional efforts to do things within my community. I'm sure that some of that comes from how I was raised with my family having everything we needed among us. I believe that you can find most of what you need in your own community. That has been proven many times in my career. Most of my films were filmed on location in Harlem and other parts of New York. There were times, when I'd be looking for things for a project, I'd be downtown outside of my community. On one particular occasion, I went looking for a screen for 20 West, only to find out it was right around the corner from us. An older gentleman told me, "Oh, you can go right down on 122nd Street and get that. That's where everybody gets their screens." All it took was a conversation with someone in my community to realize it was right there, under our noses. Most times, it is simply about asking.

Another time, I was working on a film, and I needed a courthouse. They had the cutest little courthouse in Harlem. I'm sure they've dismantled it now. It wasn't being used, so we were able to use the location to shoot our film. I didn't have to go somewhere else and spend money in their space. I was able to sow back into my community.

When I was in WNET-TV's training school, founded and directed by Peggy Pinn, I wrote my final story about garbage in the minority community. She was only going to pick two stories to highlight. Everybody in the class said, "Jessie, nobody cares about that. She's never going to pick that story." I told them, "Well, that's what I want to do, so I'm going to continue." She picked my story and one other film. My classmates were so mad, but I shot my film in the community. I didn't follow some lofty story set somewhere else. I tackled what was happening right there, and it worked. What I needed was there.

For me, downtown represented the place where a prominent number of whites lived. I still believe you can find what you're looking for to get things done, and it's not only "downtown." The things that you need are right in the community where you live oftentimes. You don't have to go out to whatever your "downtown" is. I've saved a lot of money and helped many people by following this philosophy.

Jessie Maple

COOKIES AND OTHER MONEY MAKERS

My experiences growing up contributed heavily to my desire to be independent and financially secure. Coming from a family of self-sustaining, hard-workers, I've rolled up my sleeves and worked to provide for myself and my family. I use the money now that I made back then. Sure, I could probably stop working and not produce anything, but I don't feel like that. That's not me. I like working. I like being independent, so I've kept that free spirit by exploring many other entrepreneurial endeavors, too. I describe it this way: "It makes sense to have a choice." And I've made sure that I've had choices throughout adulthood.

Desserts

In addition to film and television work, I've tried my hand at making vegan desserts. I was way ahead of the current trend, and the oatmeal raisin cookies were a hit! In fact, they were so good that they became a real business. We were in half a dozen health and grocery stores in the Atlanta area. Before long we were distributed up the east coast – New York, South Carolina, Georgia, and Florida. The retailers liked my cookies because they were homemade. The packaging was unique and homemade, so they stood out against the slickly packaged competitors on the shelf and sold well. If I'd had big manufacturing labels, my cookies would have blended in and likely not have done as well. It was an entirely separate arm of business for me. I wasn't in the frame of mind to go into the cookie business. I stopped because it became too big.

There's a creative part of Atlanta that I frequent called Little 5 Points. I used to sell my cookies there sometimes. People would see me selling and recognize me from something else. It didn't matter to me because I did it all. I like to create, and I like to make money.

Coffee Shop

The way that work was going after pursuing my case against the network, Leroy and I thought it would be smart to have something to fall back on. We knew things were tough in the freelance and contract world and would likely continue to be. We were not sure how long our turn on the blacklist would last. Leroy and I still had responsibilities to attend to. Rather than pursuing a traditional nine-to-five, we stayed committed to our community. Our quest led us to opening our own coffee shops in Harlem. We had two locations. They were located on Madison Avenue near 116th and at 110th & 5th (uptown) respectively. It was not uncommon for customers to witness Leroy and me flipping burgers and serving the drinks ourselves. The basis for everything I'd done was service to others. This was no different. Yes, we owned the coffee shop, but we still served.

In a feature story on me in a publication, one of the pictures they included in the profile was of me behind the counter. It still makes me smile to think of how the customers got a kick out of it all. It allowed us to develop a deep connection with those we came in contact with. In fact, it was my time in the coffee shop that inspired one of my most prominent documentaries, *Methadone: Wonder Drug or Evil Spirit*. Our time serving also allowed us to remain grounded. No one was higher than us; no one was lower than us. We were all equal, and I carry that philosophy with me to this day. We are all equal.

Figure 37 Serving at the coffee shop

FIRSTS

I didn't know that some of my achievements were as monumental as they were. A young lady informed me, during one of her research projects, that I was revered as the first African-American woman to produce a full-length independent film. Like so many other of my achievements, I wasn't hung up on being the first. But now that it's done, I am at the place of accepting my work for what it is. I never intend to be braggadocious; that's not my demeanor. My prime was good to me and allowed my tenacity to flourish. In 1974, I became the first Black woman to join the International Alliance of Theatrical Stage Employees (IATSE) union as a camerawoman. The year 1981 ushered in the completion of my film, *Will*, which is now recognized as the first full-length feature film independently produced by a woman of color in post-modern times. We started 20 West: Home of Black Cinema, the first Black film theater in Harlem in 1982. I was featured in magazines, newspapers, and publications of all sorts. People were writing about me all over, but I didn't always stop to take it all in. I was too busy doing the work to slow down. I'd like to believe that my efforts have paved the way for the people behind me to work just as hard but struggle a little less.

Giving Back

Whenever I've done something, it has never been to be the first. My goal has always been to be my personal best. As a result, I've achieved quite a few things along the way. However, at each experience, I took others along with me. Whether it was a family member hired to help on set or a community member cast in a role, it was important to me to help my people wherever I could. Success was never about just me as an individual. I hired a lot of people along the way. I gave many people an opportunity to get their foot in the door. Disappointingly, many of those same individuals never talk about me. Loretta Divine, to my knowledge, hasn't made mention of her work in *Will,* which was her first film. It remains one lone line on her IMDB page with few additional details.

I've come to accept the notion that, maybe, I was moving a little too fast for most people. My focus was on independent ownership and success. I truly believed that large scale success was achievable and sustainable, if we invested in ourselves and took leaps of faith. I have attained a level of accomplishment and notoriety, but I'm still the same person as when I started.

ARCHIVES AND HONORS

I was spurred by the Spirit to complete my various missions. As a result of my dedication, I have been blessed to receive many recognitions. I knew some things, but don't think I have really acknowledged the magnitude of my work until recently. I was just doing the work, not really focused on the accolades that came as a result. The seventies and eighties brought great experiences my way. The 2000s brought on what seemed to be a rebirth of my work. A better description may be that my work proved ahead of its time, or timeless, because it seemed to fit the needs of the world in modern times. From archival status to prestigious recognition, I've been fortunate enough to have my work continue to make an impact. I'd like to share some of the moments that stand out.

Peggy Pinn

As previously mentioned, Peggy Pinn founded and directed the National Educational Training for Television School. The program was sponsored by WNET for minority students in communication. I was accepted into the school and received a significant amount of my film training under her leadership.

Johnson Publications

I was featured in *Ebony* twice. In the February 1976 issue, a spread entitled "Lady Behind the Lens" was printed. The team spent several days with me, chronicling the ins and outs of my daily tasks as a camerawoman. I was recognized again in the August 1977 "The Black Woman" Special Issue in a story called "The Black Woman Today." As they covered statistics on Black women in the labor force, I was recognized for my choice of career in a profession in which Black women were relatively new.

American Film Institute

Among other honors, I was selected to participate in the prestigious Directing Workshop for Women through the American Film Institute. Each year, they would select several women to participate in their workshop. For this program, participants were given the opportunity to choose the script they wanted to work on. With the institute's approval, each filmmaker would be given $600, shooting space, free equipment usage and one month to complete a half-hour film. We were also given access to a list of Hollywood talent and technicians who agreed to partner on the films. No one on the list was Black. I took my one editor and cameraperson from New York. I selected other production people, including a sound person, from California. Some were Black, and others had disabilities. Once I completed my project and hosted the viewing, they were all eligible to be added to the list.

The Maple Crew

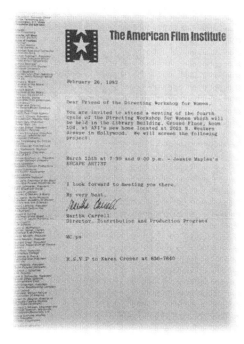

Figure 38 Invitation to my film screening

Southwestern University

In 2001, Austin's Southwestern University hosted its first annual African-American Independent Film Festival. I was the honoree at the event and had the pleasure of sharing my work with attendees. I was grateful to be recognized, not only for my specific work, but also for the doors that my work opened for others in the industry. Spelman College, Kean University and other schools have also celebrated my contributions to the industry.

Sisters in Cinema

A documentary was released in 2003 where a young sister did a lot of research to highlight the contributions of Black women in film. She shared the stories of about twenty of us, many of which have remained lesser known in the larger film world. That documentary was, in some ways, a catalyst for the revived interest in my work.

Indiana University

In 2005, I stored a large portion of my personal collection at the Black Film Center/Archive housed at Indiana University. The collection covers my career from 1971 to 1992. In addition to many of my films, they also maintain photographs, anecdotal records, and early script treatments among other items. Audrey Thomas McClusky was the director of the archive that worked with me to make sure my work was saved. She helped save my films and work from me. Her tenacity gave them a home at Indiana University to live outside of my basement. I give her much love for making that happen. I'm honored that work that I've created has a place where others can access what they need to move forward.

MOMA

In 2015, New York's Museum of Modern Art (MOMA) offered a screening of my film *Will* as a part of its "Carte Blanche: Women's Film Preservation Fund: Women Writing the Language of Cinema" film series.

Films by two other women were also shown that night as the precursor to mine.

Lincoln Center

The Film Society of Lincoln Center hosted a series entitled "Tell It Like It Is: Black Independents in New York, 1968-1986" in 2015. I was honored during the series with a program entitled "An Evening with Jessie Maple." The experience included a showing of two of my films, *Will* and *Twice As Nice*. There was also a Q&A session where I got to chat with the audience. Being covered by the prestigious *New York Times* for the entire affair was one of my dreams that came true.

Figure 39 Film Society Lincoln Center Catalog

The New York Times

In 2016, I was featured in the *New York Times* as a part of a story on women fighting to be part of the film and television industry. It was quite interesting to see the then and now photos that they included.

Additional Credits

I found out not too long ago that I have a Wikipedia page. I find it a little charming how people have tried to neatly package all the work that I've done. While there is a lot listed, there are so many other projects that I've been a part of that make me smile.

My editing apprenticeships included working on the films *Shaft's Big Score* (1972) and *The Super Cops* (1974).

A truly memorable occasion was when I was asked to direct the video for rapper Tupac Shakur's memorial service, here in Atlanta, organized and sponsored by his mother, Afeni Shakur. It was a wild experience trying to get all those hip-hop artists focused enough to complete the film in such a short time frame.

Figure 40 My press pass for Tupac's Atlanta memorial service

However, Tupac's tribute wasn't the first work that I'd done in the music industry. I had also worked with gospel superstar Vickie Winans. I was the producer for her video "Long As I Got King Jesus." I drew inspiration from my small-town Mississippi roots. Not only did I produce the video, but I handled the costuming and most of the casting. If you look closely at the beginning, you can see me as an extra. I was at my height with God giving me the energy to edit it quickly. I was doing things in the spur of the moment and adding them into the overall production concept. That's how the cow moos got in there!

New York Women in Film & Television

As recently as 2018, my work in film has been recognized. I don't know if it's the ease of access to technology and the Internet or if it is because the women's rights movement is experiencing a continued expansion. Either way, I am grateful that the conversations are being had openly, not just behind closed doors. I am honored to be revered as a pioneer and a champion of women's rights.

Jessie Maple

NEW GENERATION DAUGHTERS AND SONS

I often think about the generations that have come behind me. I have one daughter and one grandson of my own, but I see our collective sons and daughters and know that our young people need help. Our young people have so much potential, yet they get lost. I've always seen it as a part of my purpose to offer assistance where I can.

I did a documentary about single mothers. It really was kind of hard for me because the women seemed to have a hard time in relationships. I was able to help some of them, but some were getting attached to me. I told them that they couldn't do that. I let them know that they had to go out and get secure on their own. Many of the mothers did really well after our filming.

Some young people think you're trying to get in their business. Others can see the value, take it and use it. Some choose not to. I have to let it go when they don't. One of my friends said, "Jessie, you help people until they hate you. It's time for you to quit now." I just can't help wanting my people to do good.

The energy of young people keeps me young. However, I have found that, sometimes, they get so caught up in chasing the fame of the next big thing that they miss out on achieving success for themselves. When I give talks, the first question is, "How did you get to WCBS as a cameraperson?" Rather than focusing on what I built, how I built it and what could have been sustainable. I want the daughters and sons of today and tomorrow to know that success and approval aren't just achieved by working for somebody else. Achievement is not based on what mainstream or majority groups deem appropriate. Success is a personal best that extends to help and pave the way for others like you and those who come behind you. I know social media and reality television will have you to think otherwise. The best advice I can give is to work hard and do right. Fads may come and go, but true effort and art will transcend time.

Jessie Maple

WITH ALL DUE RESPECT

Many people have written things about me. I've been covered in magazines and featured in programs, and I still find myself caught between those who think I'm desperate for exposure and those who treat me as though I am not accessible. To be clear, I am neither.

I recently received an invitation to travel overseas to speak on a panel. I looked over the opportunity and gave it careful consideration. The host offered accommodations at a fine hotel, an assigned chauffer, and open access to practically the entire city. It all sounded great until they refused to pay my speaking fee. They sent gifts…scarves, cookies, etc. to woo me. The truth was, they needed diversity for their program. To be frank, they needed my Black face, but did not want to make the investment. I have stayed in amazing hotels; I have visited beautifully exotic places and had more than my share of escorts around cities, large and small, all on my own work ethic. I was offended at their audacity and declined the invitation.

Shortly afterward, I received an article that had been commissioned by a media and entertainment organization. It was sent to me, I'm sure, with the purest intentions, but the execution left much to be desired. The section that featured me contained quite an extensive detail of my work and history, but it was all canned. The details had been pulled from my archives, which are housed at Indiana University and other sources readily available across the internet. As I perused the remainder of the article, I was shocked to discover that the other subjects covered had been interviewed for their segments, including one guy I'd come up in the industry with. I felt abused and disrespected. The article was about me, but I'm not dead. I am still here. I am easy to contact, visible in my community, active, alive. They could have asked me. I would have responded.

On the other hand, there are moments when I'm honored by the reverence that is paid to my work by up and coming industry professionals. In one memorable case, a young woman was composing a research paper for her college coursework. During her research, she learned quite a bit regarding my work and history. She was so bright and enthusiastic regarding her work; I was elated when she shared one of the timelines she'd created with me on it. To have a legacy that allows others to learn and grow is an incredibly rewarding testament to all my difficult impasses. I still have a copy of that outline she shared with me in my home papers. It makes me smile to come across it every few years when I'm going through my things.

The point is, I love to tell my story. I enjoy sharing it. There's honor in what I've been through. I just don't want to be taken advantage of.

Jessie Maple

NEXT SCENES AND ROLLING CREDITS

While there is a long list of achievements credited to my name, there are still things on my list to do. One of my greatest desires is to release another film. My book, *Keisha & Bobby*, although set in previous times, I believe, delivers a timely message that will captivate audiences in a film. There's so much to share and so much to be learned from the occurrences and relationships in that story. In fact, I've already decided how I want the on-screen edition to end. I'm finally at the point in my life that I can take on only the projects that are of interest to me. Otherwise, I'm satisfied.

Rolling Credits

Over the years, I've written a lot of scripts and stories. I'm currently working to convert many of them into books so that they can be maintained for time to come. This book actually started as one of my scripts. I have to focus on one thing at a time in order to accomplish everything that I want. I stopped to do this work because I believed it was time to tell my story, beyond the beginning. I wanted to chronicle the entire journey, good and bad. People often hear of the end and glamourous parts, but they don't always get to see what it took to get there and the work it takes to go beyond it. This is the first time that I've really stopped to take it all in. As each moment came, I embraced it for what it was but kept going toward the next thing. I'm dedicated like that, to see it through to the end and then move on. This was fun and exciting. It stirred up some great memories for me. It allowed me to see myself in the ways that outsiders see me. I never set out to be famous. I never set out to be the first at anything. I just wanted to do my best and help others along the way. As I look back at it all, I truly am in awe of what I have been able to accomplish, just by staying focused. While I was able to lay the groundwork for many, there is still much work to be done.

It's 2019, and I still see many women and minorities fighting for the same rights that I was advocating for three and four decades ago. Women are still fighting for equal pay. Black men are still finding their space in the midst of discrimination and intimidation. We still have work to do. I believe there are things that I still have to fulfill. I believe I'll get to them.

I BELIEVE.

PART 4:
MY PHOTO MEMORIES

A Picture is Worth a Thousand Words

I didn't want to make a picture book, but the more pictures I reviewed, the more memories came flooding back. It was a pleasure to reflect back on some of the times and people in my life. These images tell stories including some of the ones I shared. Others offer glimpses into my world. I hope that you enjoy them as much as I did when selecting them.

Jessie Maple

Figure 41 Me over the years

The Maple Crew

Figure 42 Me at various points in my career

Figure 43 Me and Leroy

The Maple Crew

Figure 44 Me and Audrey

Figure 45 My grandson Nigel

The Maple Crew

Figure 46 Early Jessie's Grapevine Drafts

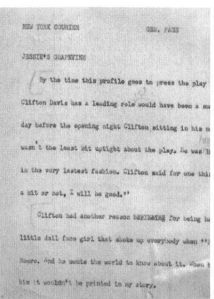

ACKNOWLEDGEMENTS – JESSIE MAPLE

With love to the following individuals: Leroy Patton, My Husband
Audrey Snipes, My Daughter Nigel Snipes, My Grandson
Fred & Peggy Lincoln, My Brother-in-Law and Sister
My Sisters – Lorraine, Diane, Debra, Camilla, Stephanie
E. Danielle Butler, My Writer

My dear friends: Kathy Anderson
John & Yolanda Bulick Winston Collymore Rochelle Davis
Paula Huys
Laura Jackson
Jessie Medlock Etta Reid
Debra J. Robinson
Craig & Velvet Walker

ACKNOWLEDGEMENTS – E. DANIELLE BUTLER

God, you do all things well. On this one, you outdid yourself!

Ms. Jessie – thank you for choosing me to walk through a beautiful lifetime of memories with you. It has been an honor to sit in your presence.

To my husband, Brandon. Thank you for letting me be. To my children, Zoe & Zachary, thank you for sharing me.

Paula! My dear friend, I can't express my gratitude enough for your encouragement and endless support in so many ways on this journey.

Christina Barnhill, Latonia Burgess, Tara Culton and Windy Goodloe – You all are the industry's best. Your labors of love are appreciated!

Lastly, to Auntie, Latrisa, Stephanie, Honey Bees and the Red Lip Society – thank you for keeping my energy high and anxiety low during this process.

I do believe in love and fairy tales!

Jessie Maple

WORKS OF JESSIE MAPLE

Books

How to Become a Union Camerawoman: Film-Videotape (1977)

Keisha & Bobby (2018)

Documentaries

Methadone: Wonder Drug or Evil Spirit (1976)

Black Economic Power: Fantasy or Reality? (1977)

Swish: Cheryl Miller (1984)

Films

Will (1981)

Escape Artists (1982)

In Search of Me (1983)

Twice as Nice (1989)

Jessie Maple

Image Index

Figure 1 My birth and childhood home 5

Figure 2 Me and my 'simmon tree 7

Figure 3 Me wearing one of my mother's suits 9

Figure 4 Mommy and me 10

Figure 5 My sister Peggy 11

Figure 6 Peggy & Fred 12

Figure 7 Me with my coworkers at the lab 14

Figure 8 My lab journal recognition 16

Figure 9 Audrey's senior yearbook page 20

Figure 10 Audrey and me 21

Figure 11 Me, Audrey, Peggy and Mommy 21

Figure 12 Leroy Patton's first photograph of me 23

Figure 13 Leroy and me 25

Figure 14 Leroy and me in 2019 26

Figure 15 Leroy & Me 28

Figure 16 My first press card 30

Figure 17 Jessie's first Grapevine article 31

Figure 18 My union card 39

Figure 19 Me carrying the camera 52

Figure 20 Me carrying the CP16 camera 53

Figure 21 Me with the camera 56

Figure 22 On the set of *Will* 63

Figure 23 On the set of *Will* with Loretta Devine 63

Figure 24 On the set of *Twice as Nice* 64

Figure 25 Leroy and me at 20 West 69

Figure 26 Bob Law 70

Figure 27 A 20 West season calendar 72

Figure 28 20 West membership form 73

Figure 29 Selling fruit outside of 20 West 74

Figure 30 Me in one of my long dresses 77

Figure 31 Carol and me at her house 77

Figure 32 Carol and me at American Film Institute 77

Figure 33 Carl Bridgers 78

Figure 34 Me as a student at Franklin 89

Figure 35 My professors and class at Franklin 89

Figure 36 Me as a short order cook 91

Figure 37 Serving at the coffee shop 96

Figure 38 Invitation to my film screening 101

Figure 39 Film Society Lincoln Center Catalog 103

Figure 40 My press pass for Tupac's Atlanta memorial service 104

Figure 41 Me over the years 114

Figure 42 Me at various points in my career 115
Figure 43 Me and Leroy 116
Figure 44 Me and Audrey 117
Figure 45 My grandson Nigel 118
Figure 46 Early Jessie's Grapevine Drafts 119

ABOUT THE AUTHOR

Jessie Maple is an American camerawoman and film director most noted as a pioneer for the civil rights of African-Americans and women in the film industry. Her 1981 film "Will" was the first feature-length independent dramatic film created by an African-American woman. She produced a second independent feature film in 1989 entitled "Twice as Nice".

"How to Become a Union Camerawoman" was Jessie's first self-published book in which she describes her challenges as a news camerawoman and becoming the first Black woman to join the union. "Keisha & Bobby" is her second book, for young adults, which she is also working towards making into a feature film.

Throughout her career, Jessie has produced short films, documentaries, and music videos.

ABOUT THE CO-AUTHOR

E. Danielle Butler is an author who has written five books and collaborated on nearly a dozen others. She has written for a number of individuals and organizations. The founder of EvyDani Books, an independent publishing house and author public relations firm, Danielle lives in Atlanta with her husband and two children.

Made in the USA
Columbia, SC
18 September 2019